American Moments

ABDO
Daughters

# MOUNT RUSHMORE

By Rachel A. Koestler-Grack

# VISIT US AT
# WWW.ABDOPUB.COM

Published by ABDO Publishing Company, 4940 Viking Drive, Suite 622, Edina, Minnesota 55435. Copyright © 2005 by Abdo Consulting Group, Inc. International copyrights reserved in all countries. No part of this book may be reproduced in any form without written permission from the publisher. ABDO & Daughters™ is a trademark and logo of ABDO Publishing Company.

Printed in the United States.

Edited by: Melanie A. Howard
Interior Production and Design: Terry Dunham Incorporated
Cover Design: Mighty Media
Photos: South Dakota State Archives, Mount Rushmore National Memorial, Forest Lawn Memorial Park, Corbis, AP/Wide World, Library of Congress, Crazy Horse Memorial, Lincoln Borglum Collection

**Library of Congress Cataloging-in-Publication Data**

Koestler-Grack, Rachel A., 1973-
   Mount Rushmore / Rachel A. Koestler-Grack.
       p. cm. -- (American moments)
   Includes index.
   ISBN 1-59197-936-6
   1. Mount Rushmore National Memorial (S.D.)--Juvenile literature.  I. Title. II. Series.

F657.R8K64 2005
978.3'93--dc22
                                                            2004062683

# CONTENTS

# SHRINE OF DEMOCRACY

Deep in the Black Hills of South Dakota stands the world's largest sculpted wonder. Four faces carved in stone gaze out over the landscape. This monument, often called the Shrine of Democracy, represents one man's vision of America. To many, the Mount Rushmore carving is a thing of beauty. To others, it is a scar upon the vast wilderness. But the monument's powerful presence makes everyone who sees it ask the same question. How did it get there?

For thousands of years, the Lakota Indians lived in and around the Black Hills. These lands are sacred to the Lakota. The Lakota believe that life is a circle from birth to death to birth again. The Black Hills are symbolic of this cycle because they, too, are a circle. A loop of red soil and rock surrounds the entire region.

In the Fort Laramie Treaty of 1868, the U.S. government promised the Lakota that they could always live in the Black Hills. This agreement set aside 26 million acres (10.5 million ha) of land in the Dakota Territory for the Lakota people, including the Black Hills. The treaty forbade whites to settle or even pass through the land.

In 1874, U.S. general George Custer led an expedition of soldiers through the Black Hills. He claimed the expedition was surveying the land. Actually, Custer intended to find out what resources were hidden in the Black Hills. Since the early 1800s, rumors of gold had spread

Tourists walk beneath
state flags at Mount Rushmore.

through the region. Custer may have wanted to see if these rumors were true.

Custer's expedition soon discovered traces of gold in the Black Hills. Before long, word of the discovery had spread. Hopeful miners swarmed the area in search of treasure. With gold fever spreading, the U.S. government tried to buy the Black Hills from the Lakota. But they refused to sell their sacred lands.

The Lakota people saw the gold miners as invaders. Relations between the Lakota and the U.S. government grew tense. Battles took place between the Native Americans and U.S. soldiers. These skirmishes escalated into war. In the end, the Lakota warriors lost. By 1877, soldiers had forced the Lakota out of the Black Hills and onto reservations. With the Lakota defeated, the Black Hills were open to white settlement.

Deep in the Black Hills, Mount Rushmore stood unnoticed and unnamed. No one could predict that within 50 years, Gutzon Borglum would come to carve the mountain's face. He would make American history forever larger than life.

*Members of George Custer's South Dakota expedition*

George Custer

# THE SPIRITED SCULPTOR

Sculptor Gutzon de la Mothe Borglum designed Mount Rushmore.  He was a talented artist, fueled by anger, energy, and an enormous ego.  His abrasive personality tested the patience of many.  But his intensity inspired others to dream.

Gutzon was born on March 25, 1867, near Bear Lake, Idaho, to James and Christina Borglum.  He never got to know his real mother.  One day, Christina called young Gutzon and his brother, Solon, in from play.  She gave them each a kiss and said good-bye.  Gutzon then watched his mother walk out the door, never to return.  Instead, Gutzon was raised by his father and Ida Michelson Borglum, his stepmother.  In 1874, the Borglum family moved to Omaha, Nebraska.

In school, Gutzon earned poor grades.  But he soon learned he had a special talent for drawing.  Often, his teachers scolded older students for not drawing as well as Gutzon.  He found drawing fun and began making sketches of horses.  Ida thought Gutzon's drawings were a waste of time.  She complained that he spent too much time scribbling pictures instead of doing chores.  She often commented, "Gutzon will never amount to anything."

By high school, Gutzon had become an accomplished artist.  Teachers and friends encouraged him to choose a career in art.

8

Fallen Warrior (Death of the Chief) *by Gutzon Borglum*

At first, Gutzon thought they were joking. But as more people showed interest in his work, he changed his mind.

Gutzon spent countless hours on his drawings. But James and Ida did not share Gutzon's enthusiasm for art. "Whoever heard of an artist . . . much less a sixteen-year-old boy, making a living," his stepmother scoffed. But Gutzon was determined to become a great artist and vowed to be famous by the time he turned 30.

In 1884, the Borglum family moved to Los Angeles, California. Gutzon was thrilled with the move. Los Angeles contained artists of all ages. Borglum tried to make a living by painting and drawing.

Unable to find steady work, James and Ida moved back to Nebraska. Borglum stayed behind and moved in with a friendly couple. He paid for room and board by painting portraits of the family members. Luckily, the couple had six children. Because Borglum could only paint in his free time, it took him many months to complete the portraits.

Before long, Borglum had earned enough money to open a studio. There, he began teaching other aspiring artists to draw. But teaching wasn't Borglum's true calling. He soon moved to San Francisco, where he met a painter named William Keith. Keith told Borglum to paint with his emotions. "When you are in a rage, is the time to paint a frothing sea, not fleecy white clouds in a calm blue sky," he said.

In San Francisco, Borglum had impressed many prominent people. But he wanted to become more well known. Many young American artists traveled to Europe to study painting and sculpture. So, Borglum sailed to Europe.

While in Paris, France, Borglum spent time with French sculptor Auguste Rodin. Rodin created the famous sculpture called *The Thinker.* Borglum was greatly impressed by Rodin's work. He decided to try sculpting.

Borglum's sculpting showed great promise. In 1891, he submitted a small bronze sculpture and a painting to the Paris Salon. The artwork at this annual exhibition was chosen by a special jury of art critics. Borglum's sculpture was of a horse standing over a dead Native American. His painting was of an American prairie scene. A few days later, Borglum received a letter notifying him that the painting had been accepted. However, there was no mention of the sculpture. Borglum was disappointed.

# AUGUSTE RODIN

*Some art critics consider François-Auguste-René Rodin to be the greatest portraitist in the history of sculpture. He was born on November 12, 1840, in Paris, France, to a poor family. Rodin entered drawing school at age 13. At age 17, however, he failed to gain admittance to the École des Beaux-Arts and became a stoneworker instead.*

*Rodin did not develop his unique style until he was in his thirties. After visiting Italy, he*

Auguste Rodin

*created the bronze sculpture* Le Vaincu *or* The Vanquished. *It was exhibited at the Paris Salon. In contrast to other works in the Salon, the statue was so realistic that some accused Rodin of molding the bronze on a living person.*

*By the time he reached 40, Rodin was famous. His body of work grew to include sculptures such as* The Thinker *and* The Kiss. *When he died in 1917, Rodin's* The Gates of Hell *was unfinished. In his lifetime, Rodin also authored three books. The most famous of these was* Cathedrals of France.

As it turned out, the sculpture had accidentally been delivered to the new National Society of Beaux Arts's salon. Famous painter and president of the new salon Puvis de Chavannes enthusiastically accepted Borglum's entry some days later.

But Borglum's success, though notable, was not earning enough money. He was over 30, broke, and not as famous as he'd hoped. After ten years overseas, Borglum decided to return to the United States. "A trip to America is just what I need," he said.

In November 1901, Borglum boarded a steamer headed for New York. He rented a studio in New York City and continued his painting and sculpting. Back home, he found a renewed desire to make a name for himself as an American artist.

Borglum created hundreds of statues for churches, including figures of the twelve apostles for the Cathedral Church of St. John the Divine in New York City. One of his most famous sculptures is a large, marble head of Abraham Lincoln, which stands in the Rotunda of the Capitol Building in Washington DC. Another sculpture is located at Gettysburg National Battlefield in Pennsylvania.

Borglum sculpted large pieces. In order to make a real impact, he thought art should have both beauty and size. He believed the early 1900s was "America's colossal age," and art should celebrate it. Often, he expressed that the United States should have a gigantic monument to celebrate the country's impact on the world.

In 1915, a southern group called the United Daughters of the Confederacy wanted a memorial of Confederate soldiers carved into Stone Mountain, 16 miles (26 km) east of Atlanta, Georgia. This granite mountain rose 800 feet (244 m) above the

Seated Lincoln

Conception

Phyllis

*Borglum sculpting*

surrounding countryside. Borglum eagerly accepted. When asked how much of the mountain he would use, Borglum replied, "The whole of it . . . I want the sky, too."

Borglum designed a large carving of famous Confederate Civil War leaders, such as Robert E. Lee, Thomas "Stonewall" Jackson, and Jefferson Davis. Behind them followed an army of Confederate troops that would span the entire surface of the mountain.

The current Stone Mountain Memorial no longer contains much of Gutzon Borglum's work. After the Stone Mountain Confederate Memorial Association fired him, it hired Augustus Lukeman to complete the sculpture. Lukeman blasted much of Borglum's carving off the mountain. He had to start from scratch because Borglum had destroyed the models. Lukeman did not make progress fast enough to satisfy the association. Stone Mountain's original owners reclaimed it from the association in 1928. Work did not continue on the mountain again until 1958 when the State of Georgia decided to complete the carving. The state hired Walker Kirtland Hancock to finish the work in 1963. Work on the Stone Mountain Memorial ended in 1972.

*The Stone Mountain Memorial*

Carving began on June 18, 1923. By January 1924, Borglum was ready to dedicate the first figure on Stone Mountain, the head of Confederate general Robert E. Lee. But Borglum's sharp temper caused problems. He got into heated arguments with the Stone Mountain Confederate Memorial Association.

The association thought Borglum was wasting their money and eventually fired him from the project. In anger, Borglum destroyed all of his models of the mountain. Members of the association were furious. They believed they owned Borglum's models and put a warrant out for his arrest.

Borglum's great Stone Mountain venture had fallen through, and he wasn't sure what to do next. He also began to struggle financially. Then Borglum received a letter from South Dakota state historian Doane Robinson. Robinson wondered if Borglum would design a carving in the Black Hills. Across the top of the letter, Borglum's assistant had jotted a note. It read, "Here it is Borglum. Let's go."

Doane Robinson

Mount Rushmore was named for a lawyer named Charles E. Rushmore in 1885. A New York businessman named James Wilson had hired Rushmore. Wilson considered investing in mines in the Black Hills. Rushmore traveled to South Dakota to check land titles in areas that Wilson's geologist favored.

While he was out with guide and miner William W. Challis, Rushmore saw a particular mountain and asked Challis its name. Challis laughed and said, "Never had any, but it has now – we'll call the . . . thing Rushmore." The mountain has gone by that name ever since.

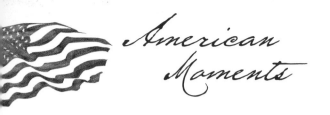

# DISCOVERING RUSHMORE

On September 24, 1924, Borglum and his 12-year-old son, Lincoln, arrived in South Dakota. The following day, Robinson took Borglum trail riding through the Black Hills. He showed the sculptor a series of thin, granite towers known as needles near Harney Park.

Robinson believed famous figures could easily be carved on the tall spires. But Borglum looked at the needles and said, "Figures on those granite spikes would only look like misplaced totem poles." They needed to look elsewhere.

Borglum returned the following year for more scouting. The rock Borglum envisioned must be massive and impressive. He wanted an ultimate challenge for his genius and to test his expert skills. Only the grandest mountain would be acceptable for his carving.

Borglum's crew spent two weeks searching the Black Hills on horseback. Then on October 1, Borglum and the others stepped into a clearing just north of Harney Park. A powerful-looking gray cliff rose into the sky. With its broad face and dramatic light, this mountain possessed the greatness he demanded.

The crew scaled the mountain. Borglum looked out over the rugged wilderness. Through incredible toil and burdens, he hoped to bring a monument the world would never forget. The party then placed an American flag atop the mountain, Mount Rushmore.

The needles form a
jagged skyline in
the Black Hills.

The location had been selected. Now, what would Borglum carve? At first, Robinson suggested western heroes, such as Meriwether Lewis and William Clark, William "Buffalo Bill" Cody, or Chief Red Cloud. Borglum disagreed. He did not want to carve just the face of some man. He felt that his grand mission was to tell a story in stone. Borglum believed this mountain should be a symbol for the nation. It must capture the spirit of democracy.

In the winter of 1927, Borglum finished the first model of Mount Rushmore. The sculpture was of three figures: George Washington, Thomas Jefferson, and Abraham Lincoln. Borglum chose these three men for the role they had played in shaping America.

Washington was the nation's first president. Jefferson, also a logical choice, drafted the Declaration of Independence. Jefferson also supported exploration of the West. He had the first visions of an America that stretched from coast to coast. Lincoln represented the United States's unity. When the country split into the United States of America and the Confederate States of America, he was willing to fight the Civil War to keep the nation together.

Borglum realized there was plenty of rock space left for a fourth head. He chose his friend and former president Theodore Roosevelt. This decision brought a flood of criticism. One argument was that Roosevelt had been dead only eight years. The other monumental figures had been a part of U.S. history for decades. Some people felt Roosevelt was not as important as the other three presidents. Others simply had their own favorite presidents to suggest.

Borglum argued that it was not the man who counted, but his role in American history. Roosevelt possessed an enthusiasm for the West. During his presidency, he set aside millions of acres of land as

*Calvin Coolidge*

national forests and parks. He also established the U.S. Forest Service. President Calvin Coolidge believed Roosevelt's effort to preserve and protect America was worthy of recognition.

Some people thought Borglum's carving was a crazy idea. One eastern newspaper joked, "Borglum is about to destroy another mountain. Thank God it is in South Dakota and no one will see it." But Borglum ignored his critics, whom he called "mere horseflies." He told his son, Lincoln, "Nothing but the hand of the Almighty can stop me from completing this task."

# THE MEN ON MOUNT RUSHMORE

### GEORGE WASHINGTON

*Known as "the Father of His Country," George Washington was the first president of the United States. He was born on February 22, 1732, in present-day Virginia. By the time he was 20, Washington had inherited the Mount Vernon plantation. In 1775, he was elected to the Second Continental Congress, which voted to break away from Britain. He served as commander in chief of the United States military during the Revolutionary War. In 1787, Washington presided over the Constitutional Convention. The various political leaders there drafted the Constitution of the United States. Washington was elected the nation's first president in 1789 and served two terms in office. He died on December 14, 1799, at his Mount Vernon plantation.*

### THOMAS JEFFERSON

*The ideals of liberty that Thomas Jefferson set forth in the Declaration of Independence have inspired many other nations, including France and China. He wrote the document when he was only 33 years old. Jefferson was born on April 2, 1743, in Shadwell in the Virginia Colony. He served in the Second Continental Congress in 1775. After the Revolutionary War, Jefferson served as the American ambassador to France. From 1789 to 1794, Jefferson became the first secretary of state. Three years later, he served as the nation's second vice president. In 1801, Jefferson became the third president of the United States. Jefferson founded the University of Virginia in 1819. He died at his home in Monticello, Virginia, in 1826.*

## THEODORE ROOSEVELT

*As the twenty-sixth president of the United States, Theodore Roosevelt expanded the influence of the United States in the world. He was born on October 27, 1858, in New York City, New York. In 1898, Roosevelt organized the First Volunteer Calvary to fight in the Spanish-American War. He emerged from the war a national hero. In the early 1900s, Roosevelt was elected vice president. The assassination of President William McKinley in September 1901, elevated Roosevelt to the presidency. In 1906, he won the Nobel Peace Prize for mediating peace talks between Russia and Japan at the end of the Russo-Japanese War. During his first term, Roosevelt arranged construction and U.S. control of the Panama Canal. In 1905, he urged Congress to create the Forest Service to preserve the country's natural resources. He died in January 1919.*

## ABRAHAM LINCOLN

*Later known as "the Great Emancipator," Abraham Lincoln hated slavery even as a child. He was born on February 12, 1809, in Kentucky to a poor farming family. Lincoln later moved to Illinois where he entered politics and became a successful lawyer. In 1858, he ran for a U.S. Senate seat against Senator Stephen A. Douglas. The candidates argued about slavery in a series of famous debates. Douglas won the election. In 1860, the two men ran for president, but this time Lincoln defeated Douglas. After the election, 11 Southern states split from the Union. This crisis prompted the Civil War. During the war, President Lincoln issued the Emancipation Proclamation. This act made liberation of the slaves an important goal of the war. Lincoln led the Union to victory. However, he did not live long enough to guide the country in peace. On April 14, 1865, he was assassinated by John Wilkes Booth.*

# CARVING A MOUNTAIN

Borglum's first big challenge was funding. Getting federal support would be difficult. Luckily, Borglum had a strong supporter, U.S. senator Peter Norbeck. For years, secluded South Dakota struggled to bring money into the state. Norbeck thought tourists would flock to the Black Hills to see Borglum's carvings. Mount Rushmore was just what South Dakota needed to bring in tourist dollars.

Norbeck convinced President Calvin Coolidge to vacation in South Dakota during the summer of 1927. South Dakota's governor quickly prepared a hunting lodge and put a sign out front that read "Summer White House." Here was Borglum's golden opportunity. He immediately planned an extravagant dedication ceremony and invited the national press to attend.

On August 10, 1927, more than 1,000 people gathered at the foot of Mount Rushmore. On horseback, the president and his Secret Service men rode to the mountain. During the ceremony, Coolidge handed Borglum six long drill bits. Borglum scaled the mountain face and began to carve as onlookers peered up from below.

In 1929, Coolidge signed the Rushmore Bill. This piece of legislation promised a federal dollar for every private dollar donated to the Rushmore project. Finally, construction on Mount Rushmore could begin.

Peter Nor

Borglum paid attention to every detail of carving. He used miniatures to test how the faces reacted to sunlight and shadows. When he perfected the miniatures, he reworked the design into a 30-foot (9-m) tall model. Even this towering structure was only one-twelfth the size of the final monument. The Mount Rushmore project made many ancient world wonders look like dwarfs. Washington's head alone was as large as the entire Great Sphinx in Egypt. In order to transfer his designs onto the granite, Borglum used an ancient Greek technique called "pointing."

*The Great Sphinx of Egypt*

*Beams used in the pointing method extend from the tops of the presidents' heads during carving.*

This system used a circular plate measured in degrees. A long retractable beam, or boom, extended out from the center of the plate. The boom could be rotated 360 degrees to measure any point on the monument.

When transferring, Borglum chose a certain point on his model. He placed the plate on top of the small model and moved the boom to a desired location. He then recorded the degree. Next, he measured how far the boom extended out from the center of the plate. Finally, he measured down from the boom to the spot he had selected.

All three measurements were recorded and multiplied by twelve. One inch (2.5 cm) on the model equaled twelve inches (30.5 cm) on the mountain. The final measurements were copied using a larger pointing system on top of the mountain. This technique told workers where to drill.

The person who calculated the points was called the pointer. The pointer had the most important job on the crew. Borglum assigned this technical task to his son, Lincoln, in 1932. Lincoln was very important to the carving of Mount Rushmore. He was 21 years old at the time Jefferson was being carved in 1933. When Borglum was in Washington DC trying to get more funding, Lincoln was in charge.

Borglum was known for his bullish behavior. One worker commented, "[He's a heck] of a stone-carver, but he ain't no sweet-talker." Lincoln offset his father's quick temper with a gift for peacemaking. He smoothed out relationships between Borglum and the workers. Borglum fired one worker more than five times. The next day, Lincoln would bring the worker back.

Borglum had to be flexible while carving his design into the granite cliff. He was constantly changing his model because of problems with the rock. It was almost as if nature had a hand in shaping his design. Originally, Jefferson was carved on Washington's right side. But after 18 months of work, the face had to be blasted away because the rock was too crumbly.

Workers started a new Jefferson head on Washington's left. In the final carving, Jefferson's face is looking up. Many people believed the reason for this position was because Borglum saw Jefferson as a visionary, a person who saw a broader America. In reality, there was a crack in the granite nose. Workers continued to tilt the head back until the crack was no longer through the nose.

Mount Rushmore workers were called the Keystone Boys. These men hung in the air at heights equal to that of a 50-story building. They were lowered down the side of the mountain on winches in special swing seats called Bosun chairs.

Lincoln Borglum dangles in front of Abraham Lincoln's face in a Bosun chair.

*Workers carve Thomas Jefferson's face.*

The pointer verified the workers' positions. Holes big enough to hold a stick of dynamite were then drilled into the mountainside. It was an exact procedure. The workers did not want to blow too much rock away and damage the area left to be carved. To bring out the faces, workers drilled and blasted 120 feet (37 m) deep in places.

After workers removed the surface chunks, they performed more delicate work called honeycombing. Workers drilled clusters of surface holes at different depths. They then chipped away small sections of granite with a tool called a channel iron. Honeycombing was exhausting work. The channel iron was attached to a 60-pound (27-kg) jackhammer. Wind made the jackhammer difficult to hold steady.

Gutzon Borglum examines the Keystone Boys' work as one of the presidential eyes is honeycombed.

Workers smoothed the surface by "bumping." They used a drill with a four-star bit, but the bit was not locked into place. As the bit rotated, it bumped the surface like sandpaper, polishing as it went.

The carving of Mount Rushmore moved along at a steady pace. By July 4, 1930, Borglum unveiled Washington's head at a special ceremony. About 2,500 people gathered to watch the unveiling. As Washington's head was uncovered, the crowd burst into a roar of clapping and whistles.

But Borglum's project soon became endangered. The stock market crash of 1929 had dealt a serious blow to the nation. Twelve million people were out of work. Poverty swept across the country. On July 26, Borglum's work on Mount Rushmore stopped because of a lack of funds.

Borglum couldn't understand how money could stand in his way. He saw Mount Rushmore as his great gift to the world. The mountain would stand for thousands of years for future generations to enjoy. Borglum felt that a gift of this size should not be measured in dollars.

Senator Norbeck again came to the rescue. In the early 1930s, when President Herbert Hoover handed out national relief money, Norbeck grabbed $100,000 of federal funds for jobs at Mount Rushmore. With money back in the Rushmore treasury, work resumed on the mountain.

Over the years, the Rushmore workers developed a loyalty to Borglum. When work stopped, they found other jobs. But when work on Mount Rushmore began again, the workers quit their jobs and returned to Borglum. The workers understood they were part of an important task. Without their dedication, the four presidential faces may not have been completed.

*Gutzon Borglum (right) stands near the Keystone Boys.*

# UNFINISHED DREAMS

Work soon began on the final face, Abraham Lincoln. Lincoln was a favorite figure of Borglum's. He had created statues of Lincoln before and had even named his son after him.

Borglum did not get a chance to finish Lincoln, however. On March 6, 1941, Borglum died of complications following surgery. He was 73 years old. After 14 years of toil, hardship, anger, and sweat, work on Mount Rushmore drew to a close.

Lincoln Borglum took over the project and finished it up as best he could. The Keystone Boys continued to show up for work every day, but the attitude on the mountain was different. Without Borglum, the project seemed to lose its drive.

Work on the monument stopped for the last time on October 31, 1941. Tools were taken apart and the models packed away. Lincoln climbed the steep stairway to the mountain peak one last time. It was difficult to leave the mountain unfinished. But Lincoln was proud of what his father had achieved. What started as the unthinkable ambition of one man had become an amazing reality.

Borglum surpassed the nation's expectations and rose above his opposition. "Don't say 'I can't' on this work," he said. "The 'I can'ts' are unknown in the world's work and unremembered in history." A South Dakota monument that supposedly no one would

*Workers carve Abraham Lincoln's head.*

*Lincoln Borglum stands in front of one of his
father's models of Mount Rushmore.*

see, now draws 2.5 million tourists a year. Since 1930, more than 50 million people have visited Mount Rushmore.

But Borglum's death left much unfinished. The original models showed all four presidents carved to the waist. In his lifetime, Borglum saw only the faces emerge from the stone. Borglum also envisioned a large timeline etched into the mountain. This entablature would document important dates in American history in 20-foot (6-m) letters. The entablature, however, was never undertaken.

Before his death, Borglum had started work on a Hall of Records. This 100-foot (30-m) tunnel into the mountain would lead to an enormous domed room. Inside, visitors could view copies of the U.S.

Constitution and other historical documents. Sixty-eight feet (21 m) of the tunnel had been drilled at the time of Borglum's death. This, too, was left unfinished.

But on August 9, 1998, a small piece of Borglum's dream was fulfilled. Sixteen panels were placed in the unfinished Hall of Records. The panels contain information about Mount Rushmore, Gutzon Borglum, and the history of the United States.

Borglum predicted that his art would be a gift to the future. He created the Mount Rushmore carving to last forever. The carving is actually three inches (7.6 cm) thicker than it is supposed to be. This extra rock allows for weathering and erosion at a rate of one inch (2.5 cm) every 100,000 years. Borglum stated that the faces will not be finished for another 300,000 years.

Still, the National Park Service works to protect the mountain. Today, at least three cracks run through the monument. These cracks could cause problems for the future stability of the mountain. One crack runs through Washington's right ear, another through Roosevelt's hairline, and the third down Lincoln's left eye. The cracks are filled with a silicone-based paste and checked every month for spreading.

Today, the world marvels at Mount Rushmore. Borglum once said, "Sheer mass is emotional." The 2.5 million tourists who visit Mount Rushmore every year would probably agree. Washington's face alone is 60 feet (18 m) tall, his nose 20 feet (6 m) long, and the slits of his eyes are 11 feet (3.5 m) wide. But the colossal carvings do more than just awe people with their size. They remind visitors of the deep pride that Gutzon Borglum felt for the United States.

The Crazy Horse Memorial is located 17 miles (27 km) southwest of Mount Rushmore. When completed, the sculpture of the Lakota chief will be the largest in the world. It was begun by Korczak Ziolkowski in 1948 at the request of the Lakota. Ziolkowski was an assistant to Gutzon Borglum during the carving of Mount Rushmore. No actual photographs exist of Crazy Horse, as he never allowed himself to be photographed. The monument is instead intended to represent the spirit of Crazy Horse and what he meant to his people. Crazy Horse's arm, in the final carving, will be stretched out. This is to represent the response he gave to a white man who asked him, "Where are your lands now?" "My lands are where my dead lie buried," Crazy Horse said.

# TIMELINE

**1867** — On March 25, Gutzon de la Mothe Borglum is born.

**1868** — The Fort Laramie Treaty guarantees 26 million acres (10.5 million ha) of land in the Black Hills of the Dakota Territory to the Lakota people.

**1874** — General George Custer leads an expedition into the Black Hills. The expedition discovers gold.

**1877** — The Lakota people are forced out of the Black Hills, and white settlers move in.

**1915** — The United Daughters of the Confederacy ask Borglum to carve a memorial upon Stone Mountain in Georgia. Borglum accepts.

**1924** — In January, Borglum dedicates the head of General Robert E. Lee at Stone Mountain. He leaves the project soon afterward.

On September 24, Borglum and his son, Lincoln, travel to South Dakota to scout a good location for another memorial.

**1925** — On October 1, Borglum decides to carve a memorial onto Mount Rushmore.

**1927** — Borglum finishes the first model of the Mount Rushmore carving during the winter.

On August 10, President Calvin Coolidge attends a dedication ceremony at Mount Rushmore.

**1929** Coolidge signs the Rushmore Bill. Carving at Mount Rushmore begins in earnest.

**1930** On July 4, Borglum holds an unveiling ceremony for the sculpture of George Washington's head.

On July 26, construction at Mount Rushmore stops because of a lack of funding. It soon resumes after a $100,000 grant from President Herbert Hoover.

**1941** On March 6, Gutzon Borglum dies from complications after surgery. Lincoln takes over construction at Mount Rushmore.

On October 31, work on Mount Rushmore ends.

**1998** On August 9, 16 panels describing Gutzon Borglum, Mount Rushmore, and the history of the United States are placed in the unfinished Hall of Records.

*American Moments*

# FAST FACTS

German emperor Frederick Barbarossa gave the Borglums' ancestor, Conrad Reinhardt, the title "de la Mothe" or "the one of courage" in recognition of his bravery in 1190 AD. During a crusade, Reinhardt saved the emperor from a wild animal. The title remained in the family.

Although the work was dangerous on Mount Rushmore, there were no deaths or major accidents in the 14 years of work. By the end of the project, workers had removed 1.5 million tons (1.36 million t) of granite from the mountain.

The Keystone Boys had a baseball team. On several occasions, the team made it to the state championships. Many workers thought they got a job at the Mount Rushmore because they were good baseball players.

Gutzon Borglum asked President Calvin Coolidge to write the inscription for the entablature at Mount Rushmore. When Coolidge did so, Borglum edited the text. Coolidge became frustrated, and eventually the text was thrown out. Later, a public contest was held to find a writer for the entablature. Although William Burkett won, the entablature was dropped from the project because the carving of Jefferson's head needed to be moved. A bronze plate of Burkett's entablature now rests on-site at Borglum's studio.

On July 4, 1991, President George H.W. Bush officially dedicated Mount Rushmore. It had not been officially dedicated before that time. The move may have been prompted by the fact that an organization was seeking to have the head of musician Elvis Presley carved onto Mount Rushmore. However, experts say there isn't enough space left for another sculpture.

# WEB SITES
# WWW.ABDOPUB.COM

Would you like to learn more about Mount Rushmore?  Please visit **www.abdopub.com** to find up-to-date Web site links about Mount Rushmore and other American moments.  These links are routinely monitored and updated to provide the most current information available.

*Visitors view Mount Rushmore*

# GLOSSARY

**civil war:** a war between groups in the same country. The United States of America (Northern states) and the Confederate States of America (Southern states) fought a civil war from 1861 to 1865.

**Confederate States of America:** the country formed by the states of South Carolina, Georgia, Florida, Alabama, Louisiana, Mississippi, Texas, Virginia, Tennessee, Arkansas, and North Carolina that left the Union between 1860 and 1861. It is also called the Confederacy. The people and soldiers of the Confederate States of America were known as Confederates.

**democracy:** a governmental system in which the people vote on how to run the country.

**erosion:** wearing or rubbing away of rock, soil, or land.

**retractable:** able to be withdrawn.

**salon:** a hall for the exhibition of art.

Secret Service: a government agency in charge of protecting the president.

silicone: multipurpose compounds made from silicon. Silicone compounds are water and heat resistant.

skirmish: a small battle in a war.

sphinx: a mythical creature of ancient Egypt or Greece that possesses a man's head and a lion's body. The Great Sphinx in Egypt was created between 2575 BC and 2465 BC. It is about 240 feet (73 m) long and 66 feet (20 m) tall.

totem poles: painted poles carved by Native Americans on the Northwest coast of the United States and Canada. These poles are used as grave markers, memorials, and for other purposes. In rare cases, a totem pole might contain a whole family legend in carvings.

winch: a machine on which a cable can be coiled and uncoiled. Winches are used for hauling or lifting.

*American Moments*

# INDEX